M IS FOR M$NEY

Written By **Rob Phelan**

Ilustrated and Designed by **Fx And Color Studio**

ISBN: 978-1-7371490-2-6 (Hardcover)
978-1-7371490-0-2 (Paperback)
978-1-7371490-1-9 (ePub)

Library of Congress Control Number: 2021938040

Printed by Rob Phelan in the United States of America.

First edition 2021.
www.misformoneybook.com

To my wife and son whom I value more than anything in this world.

Hi! My name is Stash the Squirrel.
I love saving my acorns and talking about money.

Everyone uses money in different ways and
the fun part is you get to choose your own way too.

Are you ready to learn new words about money?

Look for me on every page and try to answer my questions.

Let's go!

*A guide for how to best use M is for Money with
your reader is included at the end of the book.*

A is for ALLOWANCE

Money your family gives you that you don't have to work for.

CHOOSE Generosity

KEEP CALM and be a FINANCIAL GROWNUP

What would you do with an allowance?

*Natasha's parents give her a small **allowance** every week.*

B is for BANK

A place where you can store your money safely.

Where is the closest bank to your house?

David went with his parents to the bank to put his birthday money into his bank account.

C is for COST

How much money you need to buy something.

$1 $1 $1   20¢

How much does a banana cost?

Tina saw the cost of an orange at the store was one dollar.

D is for DOLLAR

The type of money used in the United States.

Sarena got a dollar in her birthday card from Grandma.

E is for EARN

Doing something that makes you money.

> What are some ways you can earn money?

Jasmine likes to earn money by walking dogs.

F is for FREE

Something you don't have to pay any money to get.

What is something fun you can do for free?

*Noah was excited. Someone was giving away a **free** bike!*

FREE

G is for GIVE

When you let others have some of your time, money, or things for free.

*Every week, Bailey and her parents **give** food to people who need it.*

His for HOME

**Somewhere to live that
keeps us warm and safe.**

*Homes come in all shapes and sizes.
Jamal lives in a townhouse with
his family and dog.*

How many different
types of homes can
you think of?

I is for INVEST

**When we use our time or money now,
to get something better later.**

*Suzie invests a lot of time watering her plant because
one day it will grow to be a beautiful flower.*

What is something you
can get better at with
practice or learning more?

J is for JOB

What you do to make money.

*Sam and Alex love to pretend
what jobs they will have
when they grow up.*

What job would
you like to do
when you grow up?

L is for LOAN

When someone borrows something such as toys, clothes, or money and gives it back later.

Alani offered to loan Kai her soccer ball so that he could practice at home.

Have you ever borrowed something from a friend?

M is for MONEY

What we use to buy things that we need and want.
It can be coins, paper, or on a computer.

What are three things you can buy with money?

Kiara is making a plan for her money.
She wants to buy a new toy and save the rest.

N is for NEED

Something you must have to live or survive.

MY SAVINGS GOAL
I am saving for A NEW TENT
I need to save $ 100

YOU DID IT!
$100
$90
$80
$70
$60
$50
$40
$30
$20
$10

FOOD

What do you need
to pack in your
bag if you are going
on a vacation?

*Sahil is packing what
he needs for his camping trip.*

O is for OWN

When something belongs to you. You bought it, earned it, or someone gave it to you.

Sophia is writing her name on her school supplies so everyone will know which ones she owns.

Pis for PIGGY BANK

A place to save your money at home.

Where do you save your money?

Any time Declan earns money, he saves it in his piggy bank.

Q is for QUARTER

A coin that is worth twenty-five cents.

Sammy's
Big Dream!

How many quarters would it take to equal one dollar?

When Taj checked his piggy bank, he counted five quarters.

R is for RENT

When you pay to borrow or use something.

Why Does The Stock Market Go Up?

What is something you or your family rents?

When Ara was learning to play guitar, her parents decided to rent the instrument first to see if she liked playing it.

S is for SAVE

When you keep money in a safe place to use in the future.

Ira can't wait to buy his bike!
He has been saving his money for months.

T is for TAX

Extra money we pay on things we buy and money we make.
Taxes help pay for things like roads, schools, and firefighters.

Marcus asked his moms why he had to pay **tax** *on his ice cream.*

$2

$1

What else do we pay tax on?

U is for USE

What we do with something.

Ashley and Michelle use *some of their money to buy crayons and coloring books.*

What else can you use money for?

V is for VALUE

Something important to you and worth the cost.

What do
you value?

Mark and his dads value visiting new places,
so they spend money on vacations.

W is for WANT

Anything that is not a need.

What is one thing you want and one thing you need?

Amanda looked at her mom and said,
"I really want that teddy bear. Can we buy it?"

Y is for YET

If something hasn't happened up until now, but it still can happen in the future.

What is something you want to learn more about?

"I don't know how to do it yet, but I can learn," said Pablo.

Z is for ZERO

There is nothing left.

LEARN TO
READ,
THEN
READ TO
LEARN!

SAVINGS

What else do you have zero of?

After spending all her savings on a new book, Danielle has zero dollars left in her savings.

Thank you for taking the time to share M is for Money with the curious young minds in your life. As a parent, teacher, and certified financial education instructor, my goal for this book is to help young people to build positive relationships with money. This starts by making money an approachable conversation to have at home, in school, and within our society.

For many of us, there are feelings of shame or embarrassment when it comes to talking about money, especially with our kids. By breaking these barriers down, we are helping kids to feel comfortable and confident asking questions and learning about responsible money management.

As you read this book, please remember that every person, peer group, and family handles money differently and each of us have unique relationships with our finances. I encourage you to bring your own experiences and customs into your conversations with the reader. For example, you may do all your banking digitally as opposed to in a physical bank. You may or may not have conditions or expectations for earning an allowance such as household chores.

Where you live, what you value, and how you "give" may be very different from the examples in the book and that is wonderful! Use this opportunity to discuss how everyone is different and personal finance is how you personally approach money.

I have included the following guide to help you get the most out of it with your young reader.

I hope you and your reader enjoy the book!

Rob Phelan

How to Use This Book
Parent, Caregiver, and Teacher Guide

"[Letter] is for [word] "

- Start with reading the letter and the focus word. This will help the reader begin to recognize the alphabet.
- As the reader gets older, ask them to identify the letter before reading the sentence aloud.
- Finally, ask the reader what sound each letter makes.
- Many of the words used in this book fall within the Common Core Standards for Reading at the Pre-K, Kindergarten, and 1st grade levels. This book can grow with your reader as they learn to recognize more of the English language.

Definition

- Below the "[Letter] is for [word]" statement, the definition of the word is given. Your reader may not be ready for this at their current developmental level. You can include or skip the definitions as appropriate for the reader.
- Read the definition aloud and ask the reader to explain it in their own words.
- A higher order question you can ask the reader is to identify other ways a money word might be used in other contexts. An example is the word "bank" which means something totally different when walking alongside a river, or "free" which can also mean "to release".

Mini Story

- Before reading the mini story, ask the reader to describe the illustration and what they see. Sample questions include: "What is the character doing?" "What items, people, or places do you recognize?"
- Read the mini story aloud and draw attention to the focus word. Ask the reader "where is that word shown in the picture?" Some are easier to spot than others, which also provides higher levels of challenge for the reader as they grow.
- A higher order question you can ask the reader is to tell you a different mini story where the focus word could be used.

Stash the Squirrel Questions

Stash is our loveable and money-savvy squirrel who wants to ask your young readers questions about their money habits, knowledge, and beliefs.

- Ask Stash's question and see how they respond. If you feel like you need to rephrase the question to help your reader understand, please do so.
- You should answer the question as well. Vocalize your thought process behind the answer and model how to have a positive, safe conversation around money.

Beyond the Book

- When and where appropriate, include the words from this book in your play with your child. Consider adding some resources such as play money, a cash register, and piggy bank to your child's play area.
- Pretend play common financial moments in your life such as going to the grocery store, visiting the bank, or bringing your car to a mechanic for service. Include purchasing, saving, giving, and investing scenarios.
- Point out the words in this book as they appear in everyday life. Then, encourage your child to start identifying them too.
- Include your child in age-appropriate money conversations such as: whether an item is a "need" or "want," the price of an item based on the price tag, or whether the item can be rented versus owned.
- When your child does start handling money of their own from gifts, earnings, or an allowance, ask for their help in developing the plan for how the money should be used. Encourage habits of saving, spending, giving, and eventually investing portions of all money received. This will build excellent wealth building habits in the future when the amount of money becomes larger.

Explore other recommended resources, activities, games, and books at
www.misformoneybook.com

Please share your experiences using this book with me!
I'd love to hear from you via email or social media.

✉ misformoneybook@gmail.com   𝐟 @misformoneybook   ⬛ @misformoneybook

Champions of Financial Literacy

A champion is someone who supports or defends a cause and this is a space to acknowledge the people who helped to bring this book to the world and donate hundreds of copies to schools and public libraries.

Thank you so much for your support and being a Champion of Financial Literacy for children.

Alissa Maizes from Amplify My Wealth • Amanda Phelan • Andrea, Analise, and Siena • Andrew Nippert • Ben Sykes • Bill Yount • Bobbi Rebell from Financial Grownups • Brian Feroldi, Author of Why Does The Stock Market Go Up? • Brian from Kidwealth.com • Cameron Huddleston, Author of Mom and Dad, We Need to Talk: How to Have Essential Conversations With Your Parents About Their Finances • Carol Pittner and her father Doug Nordman, Authors of "Raising Your Money-Savvy Family For Next Generation Financial Independence • ChooseFI • Cody Berman, Host of The FI Show • Dan Sheeks from SheeksFreaks • Dani Mendonsa • Declan • Ebony Beckford from Fin Lit Kids Box • Frazier Glenn • FRUGL • Genevieve, Eleanor and James Chapman • Harlan Landes from The Plutus Foundation • Jacob • Jamila Souffrant, Founder of Journey To Launch • Jane Chisholm • Jillian Johnsrud • Joe Saul-Sehy from Stacking Benjamins • Josh Overmyer • Jully-Alma Taveras from @InvestingLatina • Kelda Wilson • Kids Money Academy • Lara Dawson • Lindsay Giroux • Logan and Lakelyn Lorson • Mandy Bert • Maria from Beyond the Bank Binders • MK Williams from Author Your Ambition • Money Munchkids • Naseema McElroy, Founder of Financially Intentional • Nicole & John Fitzgerald • One Fi Day • Paul Vasey, Founder of CashCrunchGames • Paula Pant, Founder of Afford Anything • Playing with FIRE • S&C • Sam X Renick, Sammy Rabbit Kids Money Education • Shang from Save My Cents • Smart Money Mamas • Stephanie Kibler • Taylor & Megan Kovar - The Money Couple • Team Chintawat - Paul, Sarah, Isabelle, Lucia • The Fisher Boys • The Fisher Family • The Phelan Family • Thomas & Suzanne Abarca • Yanely Espinal, Creator of MissBeHelpful and Director at NGPF • Yegor Zadorozhnyi